Simply Wild

Luke Brannan

Copyright © 2025 by Luke Brannan

Library of Congress Control Number: 2025914963

ISBNs (all formats):

Ebook: 979-8-218-73237-0

Paperback: 979-8-218-73238-7

Dedication

For the ones who've ever felt lost in their own skin, unsure of where they belong or who they're supposed to be.

For the quiet thinkers, the overfeelers, the ones who care a little too much and can't always explain why.

This is for you.

And to the late-night drives, the unfiltered laughs, and the people who reminded me that I didn't have to be perfect to be loved — thank you.

You made me feel like I was enough, even when I couldn't see it myself.

Acknowledgment

This book wouldn't exist without the conversations that cracked me open and the people who stood by me as I tried to make sense of it all.

Thank you to my closest friends — for the midnight drives, the long talks, and the way you reminded me that being real will always matter more than being right. You helped me find the words by letting me be myself, even when I didn't have the answers.

To those who challenged my thinking or made me uncomfortable in the best ways — your voices live in these pages too.

To my readers: if this book finds you in a moment of confusion, doubt, or longing — good. You're not alone. May you walk away a little less afraid to feel it all.

And finally, to the version of me who almost gave up — this one's for you. You stayed. You kept going. You turned the mess into meaning.

Table of Contents

About the Author

Luke Brannan never set out to write a book. He's just someone who started asking questions — about life, expectations, and what it really means to feel alive. A college student and first-time author, Luke grew up watching people chase all the "right" things, only to feel like something was still missing. After facing his own struggles and periods of uncertainty, he began to realize that maybe we're not meant to have it all figured out.

Simply Wild came from those moments — quiet nights, honest conversations, spontaneous drives, and the raw thoughts that never made it into daily life. It's not about being an expert. It's about being honest. Luke doesn't claim to have all the answers, but he hopes that through these pages, readers find a little freedom to question things, embrace the unknown, and live a little more boldly, even if it gets messy along the way.

This book is for anyone who's ever felt out of place in a world that tells you to follow the script. Luke's still figuring things out too — but maybe that's the point.

Before We Begin: Grabbing the Bull by the Horns

Hi, I'm Luke, and honestly, I have no idea what I'm doing here.

The concept of this book was brought up a while back when I was looking up at the ceiling of my bedroom. Quite a bit happened back in December — loss and grief and sickness and a whole load of drama I barely knew what to do with. It all hit me at once. It was kind of wild. And then it clicked, like a lightbulb flicking on over my head.

"Wild" — that word has always stuck with me. It describes life perfectly in all its unpredictability.

So, I decided to take a shot in the dark and see where my limited writing skills and overactive mind could take me. What ideas would open not just my mind but the reader's?

I'm not a great writer. In fact, I usually avoid it because organizing my ADHD thoughts feels like trying to untangle a mess of wires. It's overwhelming. By the time I finally sort everything out — if I even get that far—an hour or two has passed before I've written my first word.

I start a lot of projects and hobbies but rarely finish them because I get too distracted. And yeah, I make a lot of mistakes in writing, and I can't tell you how long some of these paragraphs took me.

I found inspiration in *The Subtle Art of Not Giving a Fck** by Mark Manson. Not to copy his style, but to learn from it. My goal was to challenge myself, to push past my limits, even if it meant spending hours and hours thinking and rewriting.

Now, my next goal? To be able to write like this naturally — to take my own advice about embracing the wildness of life.

I hope this book inspires you to do the same. Take the bull by the horns. Take risks. Go after something greater.

Be simply wild.

Introduction

We can feel how unpredictable life is. No one actually knows what they are doing. Yet we all pretend that we do — we roll through the motions. We fight, steal, work jobs we hate, and spend years earning a degree that may or may not be worth it, all while caught in this whirlwind.

It's a burden for anyone struggling day by day to keep up with the expectations of others — and often those we apply to ourselves.

But why does it have to be this way?

Society gives us a checklist: go to school, finish college, get a job, work, retire, and then what? What's the endgame? And why does it feel like we're just moving on this treadmill, running faster but not really going anywhere?

Robin Williams once asked, *"What do you want to do?"* And to be honest, that is a damn good question.

It's like being given a map, but not everyone is meant to follow the same path. How many of us feel disconnected from the life we were taught to live? You've likely had moments when you stopped, looked around, and thought, *"This is really all there is?"*

That deep feeling in your core — something isn't matching up with the story you were told to lead.

That's what I question here. I want to step off the beaten path of daily life and consider something different: Is a life beyond the assembly line of expectations really so bad? Does it really hurt to face the uncertainty, to question the life we've been so accustomed and trained to live by?

What if it's meant to be wild, unpredictable, and just different? What are we denying ourselves by sticking with a "safe" routine?

How many of us have found ourselves stuck in cycles we didn't fully choose for ourselves? What is taught in our minds is what children receive in life: go straight from school to university and then into the sort of job you intend to keep forever. Your entire life will follow a predetermined path.

But what if life can't be like that for everyone?

This book isn't here to provide you with the answers. It intends to shake things up — make us question why we do things, and just what really counts in life. It is about figuring out how one travels on through life without losing sight of who they really are in the process.

So come on, let's dive in — let's discuss what makes life wild, and why maybe that isn't such a bad thing after all.

Chapter One
What on Earth Is Normal?

Since we were children, we have constantly been told to be "normal." What on earth does that mean?

"Normal" can vary so widely depending upon one's culture and position in society. In some places, being lively and open is normal; in others, being introverted or silent is considered right.

While women today are encouraged to pursue careers, there's still a lingering expectation that they also excel in homemaking — often placing double pressure on them to "do it all." What was unnatural fifty years ago may be quite understood now, and vice versa.

"Normal" is really only a tribute to conventional standards, beliefs, and customs. Essentially, it means following the rules — and this is where the challenge lies. When we always try so hard to fit ourselves into someone else's shoes, we lose sight of who we are.

Yet the irony is that we fail to see this: some unseen force tells us that normal is the only way to succeed, and we willingly fall in line.

However, in the process of blending in, life becomes extremely predictable — and boring. We go through the same routines every day, speak with the same people, wear a lot of different clothes — but it's all part of the same pattern.

For instance, when everyone is going in the same direction, nothing interesting happens. Life may be peaceful or even simple. But is that a complete life?

No firsts, no changes — no surprises at all. There's no real meaning behind it — just a crowd of people moving all at once, to the same rhythm.

When you go with the flow, you simply become a small part of a much larger system. You do what you have to do; that is all.

The problem that follows lies with trying so hard to be just like everybody else: we are all capable of doing something different; we just refuse to remember it.

There's, after all, a pressure to be what others expect you to be. Simba, the once-heir to the throne in *The Lion King*, fled from his responsibilities following the death of his father. Racked with guilt and terror at his weakness, he deserted not only his kingdom but the burdens that he carried. He was living the carefree life of one who has no responsibilities, because stepping back into his role meant reality, pain, and being overshadowed by the past.

But eventually, he came to know that fleeing who you are doesn't bring peace. He needed to confront the past to progress. Simba wasn't just returning to Pride Rock to reassert his birthright—he was doing so on his own terms, to claim it as his own. And that changed everything.

***

But is "normal" even real? Could it be that the only prison we're in is the one we build for ourselves trying to "fit in"? Or rather, that there is no fitting in at all, but we are simply conditioned to think there is, so we stay within social bounds?

The idea of "fitting in" might just be a social construct — carefully designed to ensure we stay neatly tucked into the boxes society has created for us, preventing us from stepping outside the lines and exploring the unknown.

In reality, the people who have changed the world — scientists, artists, rebels — were never "normal." They always shook things up. They dared to be different, to write their own rules — regardless of how the majority viewed them. They pushed boundaries and resisted confinement. Had they conformed early to tradition, we wouldn't have electricity, the internet, or music that touches your soul. In short, none of the innovations that make life richer would exist.

So why do we need normalcy here? Should we spend all our lives doing what we think we should do — what is expected of us — without ever considering what we actually want or need, who we are, and what makes us happy?

The answer is no, of course.

Rather than spending more time trying to fit into a mold not made for us, we can start enjoying the weird, the unexpected, and the different.

Going Deeper into the Challenge of Normalcy

However, escape from the usual is never simple. The fear of rejection is ferocious, and the pressure to fit in is intense. Many times, those expectations were internalized from the moment we were kids — parents, teachers, friends, and sometimes strangers showed (or didn't show) us how to act.

Statements like: *"Why can't you just be like us?"* or *"Don't rock the boat,"* pressure people to conform.

Deep down, we long to break free — to choose our own path and live authentically.

For instance, take a person who was raised in a household where having good grades was the top priority. They may have spent the past few years living a life shaped by others' expectations—to work hard, get good grades, and then attend a selective college. But they may have always aspired to be an artist, a musician, or a traveler.

These loves may have been dismissed or ridiculed by their family as unrealistic. Through that process, such a person might have buried their own inner calling, buying into "normal," which promised status and success.

But what do you do when someone eventually shows up and dares you to question normal?

Maybe they're a little homesick, for a start. At the beginning, there is an adjustment period where one feels lonely, questions their decisions, and fears that trying something new could make things worse.

But eventually, they could discover lives that feel more authentic — even as everything else seems to fall apart.

Well, it's rewards after taking risks.

Why the Strange Should Not Terrify Us

When we move away from the ordinary, it's important to remember that change takes time. It happens slowly, in small steps, before it transforms into something new.

Some might think you're a little silly wearing a graphic T-shirt with a fun, bold message on it, but for you, it might represent something deeper — your journey to genuineness. What others consider trivial might well turn out to be something critical — or life-altering — for you, and represent the shift from doing what you believe you should do, into the realm of doing what you feel you must do.

This small act of resistance can spark a great feeling of freedom. It's here, in thinking daringly different, that the seeds of real innovation may be planted. A scientist who challenges the common beliefs, an artist who isn't chasing trends, a business leader with the courage to question outdated ideas and propose something new.

In fact, some of the most iconic characters in storytelling were seen as outsiders or misfits in their own worlds.

Think of Shrek, who lived far from the kingdom and was constantly judged for who he was. Instead of trying to blend in, he owned his identity and changed how others saw him.

Or take Tony Stark — Iron Man — who defied military expectations and corporate norms by dismantling his weapons empire to build a future powered by innovation and accountability.

They didn't fit the mold, and they didn't try to. Instead, they reshaped it entirely.

We need a lot more thinking like this now. So it is urgent that there are more people unafraid of the future. With fresh thoughts in their heads and on their tongues (never fearful of voicing them), they tackle obstacles headfirst and live in truth.

The less normal we want, the more the world bursts open with potential.

Embracing the Unusual Is a Challenge

As long as it seems "weird" to you, whatever you do doesn't need to be bad. It could be as small as wearing two different-colored socks every morning, or letting out a loud hum while walking downtown in public.

What about walking up to a stranger and having a deep talk with them? What does that feel like — stepping outside your comfort zone? What is the effect on those around you — do they smile, look confused, or even judge you based on their own standards of taste and what they think you should understand or appreciate?

What is it like for you — liberating, awkward, exciting, nerve-wracking... or what?

When the time comes, consider how these rare experiences made you feel and what you did in response.

Imagine if you were able to do this all the time — if everyone just let go of society's stereotypes and lived their life. If you didn't have to be "normal," then what would your life look like?

Consider the possibility that these little rebellions could be empowering. They are tiny steps upon which a real life is made.

Get out of your comfort zone, and you will slowly shatter the fallacies of the norm.

Look forward instead.

Chapter Two
Always Chasing More

It feels like we're always after something more—the next phone, the next job, the next big win. There is always something on the horizon that holds out hope of happiness, fulfillment, or success. Got that, and we will at last feel whole.

"I'll be happy if I get there."

But the moment you get there, you'll realize the "next thing" is already waiting for you, just out of reach. So you keep moving on — never satisfied, never quite reaching wherever it is we want to go.

This is desire's endless cycle. New trends, new opportunities, new beginnings. It's like getting the new high-speed pursuit of these things has become our natural state of affairs. The problem is not in wanting more; the problem lies in thinking that *more* is the only road to happiness.

Accumulated wealth and increased status — we have been conditioned to regard such things as the keys to happiness. However, the truth is that happiness can never be found in any "next big thing."

Happiness is often seen as something in the future, waiting for you to reach it after hitting one target after another. Rather, happiness exists in *this* moment — the moment you are currently working to make better, right here, right now. This moment, flawed and uncertain as it is, is enough.

But we are also inclined to ignore it, eternally focused on the next moment just around the corner. There's certainly nothing wrong with having goals and pursuing self-improvement. But when we say to ourselves that we'll be happy or content or satisfied *when* we achieve those goals, then we are always chasing something that's just out of reach — a never-ending cycle. We're so concentrated on the future, we forget to live in the present.

Take a moment to really think about the people around you. The last time you genuinely experienced them in your heart — not because they gave you something or worked you into achieving some outcome, but primarily due to who they are?

Often we associate happiness with some great accomplishment or new things. But real happiness lies in life's little moments — those plain, ordinary moments where nothing out of the ordinary really happens.

It is nights like those — the kind when you sit with friends in a room until the early hours of the morning, laughing until your stomach hurts. It's those jokes you share with friends that only make sense to you and nobody else. It's all of that shared experience that is so intimate no outsider could begin to comprehend. It is these things that remind us what life is really about — not some grand gesture or a fancy trip around the world.

Author's Note

I remember those nights I would just jump in my friend's car — no plans — and cruise around the village. McDonald's at midnight, just talking about random stuff, laughing at nothing and everything.

It wasn't anything fancy. No big plans or special reason — just enjoying each other's company and living in the moment. Honestly, some of my best memories are from those late-night drives.

And because we're not always paying attention to today — if we are always concentrating on the future instead of what is going on now — we'll lose sight of what we already have.

Even when life points us toward the future, the goal isn't to abandon all effort or ambition, but more about how to really feel good about the process that you're in, right now, instead of waiting for something off in the future to make you happy.

The world offers so many distractions, and all too often our minds just want more and more, thinking that once we have it, everything will be okay. When in fact, there will always be another thing to strive for. And thus the circle goes on — we chase success, approval, or security — until we finally realize we were striving for the wrong thing all along.

Success can be both reality and illusion. For example, social media is actually a breeding ground for this problem. Every time we pick up our phones nowadays, it's hard not to come across pictures of perfect holidays, brand-new cars, luxurious garments that seem more like works of art than clothing — all in a world without any problems at all.

We observe other people enjoying life to the fullest, and thus we start to doubt our own existence.

"Why can't I have what they have?" we ask ourselves.

Sadly, not everything is told by these images. People only let you see their high points. What they do is dress things up and show you only a side that is unadulterated pleasure. But it does not show the messier, less glamorous side of life — a shattering disappointment here, an embarrassing setback there.

Social media nowadays depends on idealized life, though, and when you are scrolling through a stream of other people's edited experiences all day long, a lot goes unnoticed.

When we believe that everyone else has it better than we do, we forget that appearances aren't always the reality. It's easy to look at others' successes and feel like we're falling short, but each of us has our own path to follow.

The problem is not wanting more. It's that we define our happiness in terms of what we don't have.

True happiness isn't something that can be bought or earned; it's something that already resides within us and grows by embracing the present moment. When people let go of this belief that happiness is something waiting to happen in the future, then they will begin to find it happening today and now, right where they are.

The Appreciation Pause

Action: For the next five days, begin or end your day by writing down three things that make you feel grateful — no matter how big or little.

It doesn't take much to be grateful for something: a warm cup of coffee in the morning; the sun on your face; a conversation with friends over lunch.

Try to write and then take a pause while considering your gratitude list. What does it feel like when you focus on what you have, instead of what you don't?

Notice how your perspective shifts. Rather than always thinking about what's coming next, you may begin to notice and appreciate what you already have right here and now in front of you.

Reflection

_____

_____

_____

_____

_____

_____

_____

Chapter Three
Politics Is All A Show

Politics used to be about ideas and debate. At its core, it was meant to be a space where people could come together, share opinions, criticize one another, and, ideally, work toward a common good.

But now, it feels more like a TV show or reality game. It seems that politicians have become celebrities, with their actions now part of a binge-worthy show. Every news channel, social feed, and even casual conversation revolves around analyzing their moves.

What used to be meaningful is now all about the spectacle. Folks take sides like a sporting event — they cheer for their "team" and attack the other side.

It's more about shouting than having a real discussion — more about defending positions than exploring the soundness of counterarguments. And in that environment, serious debate becomes all but impossible.

Author's Note

I've tried to have political conversations where I stayed calm and open to hearing both sides. But more often than not, it felt like the discussion was one-sided, with no real effort to listen or understand.

Instead of exchanging ideas, it felt like I was being dismissed or generalized.

It's tough when you try to engage, but the conversation doesn't go beyond surface-level defenses.

In the few conversations where both sides listened, I felt like we made real progress — and that's the kind of dialogue we need more of.

***

Politicians make promises — some of which they actually fulfill — while others engage in empty gestures. Then, they break those promises with little to no consequences.

Yet they don't just get away with these betrayals — they seem to keep the trust of their supporters.

It's as if we are forever forgiving our disappointment, forever ready to let any lies or mistakes slide because we know the characters so well.

But isn't that the point? They know how to play the game.

They understand that political loyalty is not just about policy — it's about narrative.

It's about establishing loyalty and belonging.

And because so many of us are caught up in this narrative, we fail to ask the hard questions or accept anything less than what we deserve.

Worst of all? Most of us aren't even really discussing the issues anymore.

We have become so distracted by the drama.

We get so caught up in the headlines and exaggerated stories that we stop focusing on the real issues.

Instead, we just repeat what we read online, what's on TV, what's in someone's social media post — spouting talking points like robots, without trying to understand the complexities of issues.

In a sense, we have become puppets, shaped by the stories told by those in power.

And who benefits from that? The ones in charge.

They want us to be divided and fighting with each other over nothing, so we will all go our separate ways and not even register that they're making decisions about our lives that will affect us in ways we can't even imagine.

The distractions are intentional — smoke and mirrors to keep us from looking too closely at what's really going on behind the scenes.

***

The world is chaotic, and politics might be even messier.

It's not simple, it's not a straight line, and it's often infuriating.

But if you're not paying attention to what's going on around you, someone else will make all the decisions for you — and that's a fate worse than simply watching the show unfold.

When we disconnect, we ignore our responsibility to ourselves and others.

We end up living in a way that's not true to who we are, and in the end, we lose the chance to shape our own story.

The longer we stay comfortable, the more the current system stays in place, making it harder to bring about real change.

***

Surrounded by the chaos and noise of politics, it is easy to feel powerless.

The options can seem limited, and the consequences overwhelming.

But that's exactly what political systems rely on — making us feel stuck and powerless.

But we cannot afford to sit and do nothing.

Change begins with awareness of what's really happening, asking difficult questions, and demanding better from the systems that hold us back.

And although politics may seem like a distraction these days, it's one that we can do something about — if we stop watching and start acting.

The Challenge: Have a Real Debate

Get to know someone who holds a different opinion than you about a political or social issue.

Try to understand their perspective, and instead of arguing, simply ask:

"Why do you think that?"

Allow them the space to express their opinion without interrupting, while trying to put yourself in their shoes and feel the way they're seeing the issue.

Then, mirror their point back so they know you heard and understood.

Only after you've fully taken in their point of view should you offer your own.

The point of this exercise isn't to win a debate — it's to build understanding.

In a divided world, simply listening can be a powerful act of resistance.

Practice, and notice how it alters your response not only to the problem but to people around you.

You might find that the "sides" we so often take are not as black-and-white as we think, and the true work lies in our shared experiences — in showing compassion and respect toward one another.

Chapter Four
Making Chaos Work For You

Life is unpredictable. Despite how much you plan, prepare, and do to ensure that everything goes according to your plan, life has a funny way of throwing curveballs. Not everything goes the way you want it to. But you know what? That isn't necessarily a bad thing.

Imagine this: when alarms go off, you don't freak out or panic. What if, instead of automatically identifying yourself as a failure, you took a step back and realized that the shortcomings are just part of the path you are on? What if the chaos wasn't something to fear or run from, but something you could learn to work in your favor?

The chaos can be turned into an advantage in three easy ways:

1. **Stop stressing out over what you should do.** We get hung up on the belief that there's a certain way that life is "supposed" to go. We're concerned that we'll fall off course, that we need to do something else, or that we've overlooked an important step. But here is the truth: there is no perfect script to life, and the messy parts — the moments you didn't plan for — are often what lead us to the greatest growth. Just release the pressure to know everything.

2. **Your expectations will never match reality.** Flexibility is key. You don't have to be naïve and think life is going to be super smooth — it's not — but instead of viewing challenges as a signal that you're failing, view those challenges as opportunities to innovate, learn, and adapt. You are resilient not due to the ability to plan your moves, but rather because of the flexibility to readjust

your steps when things don't go your way. It's not about clinging to a path but discovering new routes when the old ones are not working.

3. **Keep in mind that failure is not final — it's just another step forward.**

   Many people believe they must avoid failure no matter what. But failure isn't the reverse of success — it's part of the process. You learn each time that you fall down. You learn what doesn't work, and that gets you one step closer to learning what does. So when plans go awry, don't consider it the end. It's a lesson and part of your process.

Life is not a perfect plan that always pans out. It's about finding the ability to regain momentum when things don't go as planned. Because guess what? Things will go awry, and that's living. Those challenges are part of a bigger journey, shaping and strengthening you.

What causes some people to persevere when others quit? It isn't talent, luck, or perfection. It's resilience.

Rocky Balboa put it best:

"The world ain't all sunshine and rainbows. It's a very mean and nasty place, and I don't care how tough you are, it will beat you to your knees and keep you there permanently if you let it.

You, me, or nobody is gonna hit as hard as life. But it ain't about how hard you hit, it's about how hard you can get hit and keep moving forward.

How much you can take and keep moving forward.

That's how winning is done!"

That quote may sound like it's about boxing, but it's really about life. Life is tough. It will take you down, time and again, and you'll feel the wheels coming off. You'll sometimes feel like a total failure. But the key, as Rocky

24

would say, isn't dodging the punches. It's about the way you pick yourself up after life knocks you down again and again. That's how you move forward. That's how you win.

I think too many people spend too much time complaining about what they don't like in their life — the bad luck, the things in the way, the people that have done them wrong. But guess what? Whining doesn't make a difference. It's what's next; it's what you do with that; it's what you learn from it.

Exercise: Embracing Setbacks

Identify a challenge or failure in your life recently. Perhaps it was something minor, or perhaps something that felt very big. Now, jot down three lessons from that experience:

1. How did it make you stronger?
2. What did it reveal that you wouldn't have seen otherwise?
3. What did you learn from this failure that helped you grow?

Reflection

_____

_____

_____

_____

_____

_____

Embrace your setbacks. They are the starting point for something better. Every failure is a lesson learned. This is not about how hard you fall — but how you get up and how you keep going.

Chapter Five
Identity Crisis

In psychology, what stands out to me most is **Social Identity Theory**. As you can gather by the name, it gives an explanation of why we are often, in general, quite similar to those around us. This is to say, with reference to the containing groups we all belong to — families, friends — those places can then shape not only how we see ourselves but also how we expect others to behave around us, or what is acceptable behavior on their part.

Check for yourself: even if we don't consciously recognize it, the roles we hold within these groups influence how we see ourselves and shape the way others interact with us and respond to our behavior.

This isn't inherently a bad thing. Everyone wants to belong somewhere. When we are part of a group, we have an identity and relationship. It helps us locate others who share our values and beliefs. That makes it easier for us to understand where we stand in relation to others. There is comfort in being with others who are like you.

But the problem comes when we over-identify with a group and its role.

When we over-identify with one side, the relationship becomes one of **"Us vs. Them."** We become focused on defending our own views, with no room for negotiation or even a genuine attempt to listen to others. It's as if we've already decided that our point of view is the only valid one, and we dismiss any further input, assuming they have nothing valuable left to say.

So instead, we let the crowd think for us without any thought on our part, and allow our assumed role as a member of that group to determine how we look at things. In politics, in sports, or in any social issue, how often do people take one side or the other simply because it is their own team? They trouble to support it regardless of what rational argument there may be against it — just because that defines them.

This is related to another cognitive bias: the **Fundamental Attribution Error**. This is the tendency to explain other people's mistakes as a reflection on their personality, but when we make our own mistakes, we tend to blame external circumstances for them.

Here's a practical example:

Debbie and Mandy are both trying new jobs. One day, Debbie is late. Mandy thinks, *"She is so lazy, always irresponsible."*

Yet the next day, Mandy is late, but she thinks, *"That was not my fault at all. There was just too much traffic ahead."*

Why does this happen?

When we see others make mistakes, we often attribute it to their internal qualities — so and so is careless, disorganized, or perhaps just does not have things together. But when we ourselves make a mistake, we tend to externalize it to something outside our control — like bad traffic, a rough night's sleep, or simply anything but us.

This bias is seen everywhere in day-to-day life:

When an unknown driver cuts across our lane, we say he (or she) is a bad driver. Yet if we should cut off someone else, it might be because *they simply did not see us*.

If one person fails a test, we conclude that he did not study enough. If *we* fail, it's because the test was too hard or we were just having a bad day.

When one co-worker is late with a project, it might be that she is disorganized. Should it happen to *us*, it is simply because our schedules are too full.

This is an easy pit to fall into — a way we have of upholding our own image while holding others to higher standards. We allow ourselves flexibility but are strict with others.

Author's Note

One of the hardest things I've had to do is face my own biases.

I remember a time when I met someone who seemed very different from me — different background, different values. At first, I found myself judging them. They were loud, opinionated, and unapologetically brash, which made me think they were rude and unrefined.

But as we talked more, I started learning about their experiences, their upbringing, and why they held the views they did. It turns out, their brashness came from years of being dismissed or ignored in their own life.

The more I got to know them, the more I realized how unfair I had been. I had quickly written them off based on my own biases and judgments — nothing more than surface-level assumptions.

It was a tough pill to swallow, realizing I'd fallen into the Fundamental Attribution Error: blaming their behavior on their personality instead of understanding the circumstances that shaped it.

But that moment — when I allowed myself to be open and challenged my own biases — changed my perspective entirely.

***

This creates a divide between **'us' and 'them,'** between **'the right way' and 'the wrong way,'** a gap that in fact could often better be described as more complicated, with everyone being both good in some respects as well as bad.

For example, when combined with the Fundamental Attribution Error, Social Identity Theory measures not only *who* one is, but also *what* he or she does. This picture helps explain why other people often seem to act in ways we find difficult to understand.

We identify with certain groups and then view everything through the lens of this affiliation. We neatly classify people — or, in extremes, label them "evil" as a means of getting rid of them. We justify all contrary evidence with illogical reasoning — *"They must have hit me first."*

Bad news is, when we become aware of these thought patterns, we then have the opportunity to challenge our own biases.

If addressed and corrected in our thinking, these prejudices can be dismantled. This will allow us instead to see the world as it really is — not merely what our identity has fixed it as.

Challenge: Self-Analysis

Spend a few moments in thought. List the terms you use to define yourself — student, artist, introvert, and the like.

For each label, ask yourself: *If I didn't have this tag, would I still be myself?*

Do your labels really make up your identity, or are they simply a convenient way of shelving yourself?

Consider how your self-perception would change if any of these labels were taken away. Would you still feel this is you? Or would it force you to deal with a deeper core of yourself that is not tied to external standards?

Reflection

_____

_____

_____

_____

_____

_____

_____

Chapter Six
Break The Wall Down

In most cases, the expression goes, *"When your back is up against the wall, the only way to go is forward."* It sounds so reassuring — don't stop moving forward, keep grinding away, and never mind who stops or what stands in your path.

In essence, what it suggests is that the approach to solving a tough spot is to push harder; any difficulties ahead can be overcome with sheer effort.

But suppose you can't go forward? After years of relentless struggle, no matter how hard you try, the obstacles remain. What then?

Here's an example: tear down the wall.

Who says you have to be bound by a plan? Who says you must accept the limits set by life, society, or even yourself? So many of us grow up with the feeling that, in order to succeed, we must keep moving forward along a planned route.

Yet, in fact, walls don't imprison people; they test whether these same individuals will break through them. Yes indeed, they are tests — but also invitations to leap out of the box and to be creative. It's a way to overcome the challenge from a different angle.

Every successful person, whether in business, sports, painting, or life, has to face obstacles. Some people get stuck and give up; they accept the walls in front of them. They didn't go forward by chance — but chose some other path: altering the rules, changing plans, or just refusing to take "no."

Such is the real power of endurance, which is not just the ability to stick at it, but also to redefine success when traditional paths are no longer an option.

As you may find out, your work may feel like a deadly vacuum that forces you to show up day after day, year after year. Maybe school seems like a detour — a waste of time until you can find something more meaningful to do.

Probably your personal life is a mess — relationships strained, your sense of self gone, and nothing seems to be going right. The wall is real, isn't it? You're banging up against it.

But here's the thing: You don't have to keep "moving forward" on one straight road. You can turn around, change the system, or make your own completely new path. And though it may not follow tradition, it will be genuine.

When facing a block, most of us feel we must choose between fighting through it or giving up altogether. But there's a third option — **creativity**.

If you stop for a moment to step back and re-evaluate the situation, often you'll find that the path forward is not always the best way.

What if, instead of wondering how to overcome the wall, your job was to go over or around the big thing completely?

The most successful people do not always take the straightest route to success — or ask the same questions, for that matter. Consequently, they find new paths to walk and take challenges that have never been tried before.

Author's Note

I remember a time when I was stuck in a situation that felt like a brick wall. It was a point in my life when I had been working hard at something that seemed to take all my energy — whether it was school, a job, or a personal goal.

No matter how much effort I put in, things didn't seem to move. There was no progress, and the harder I pushed, the more I felt like I was running in place.

For a while, I thought I just needed to push harder, to work longer, to try more of the same. But it wasn't working. I found myself exhausted, frustrated, and questioning if I had what it took to get past it.

And then one day, I hit a point where I realized "*I had been trying to move forward the same way, expecting different results.*"

I had built my own wall around the situation, thinking it could only be tackled by one method. But then, a shift happened. Instead of pushing against the wall, I stepped back and asked myself, "*What if I don't have to do it this way?*"

That's when I saw the opportunity to break the wall down in a completely different way.

I chose to step sideways instead of trying to climb over it. I reached out to people I never would have considered asking for help, tried methods that seemed unconventional at the time, and gave myself permission to fail without it defining me.

Slowly, the wall that had once seemed impenetrable started to crumble — not because I pushed harder, but because I allowed myself to see it as an opportunity for change, not a limit.

***

But the truth is that walls are only an obstacle for people who accept them. As soon as you believe that a wall is an unstoppable force, it becomes one.

On the other hand, if you see them simply as another challenge to be met or an invitation for new routes and possibilities, then their power withers away.

When life stops being just up and down, and starts also taking off sideways, see the wall not as a limit, but as a chance to think freely and break from convention.

The whole world is full of walls — but there are also means to tear them down. And sometimes, coloring outside the lines is just a matter of deciding, *"I can."*

Exercises: Spot the Walls

Identify a major obstacle in your life — something that feels like it's holding you back or keeping you stuck.

Now, come up with at least **three unconventional methods** for overcoming it. Give at least **one out-of-the-box idea** a chance of winning.

Try something you haven't tried before. What's a way that might seem risky, unconventional, or even go as far as being uncomfortable to try — but could bring the breakthrough we all need?

Think courageously and imaginatively — not only to solve the problem, but so you finally get rid of the idea that you have no way out.

If you believe that life can have this kind of freedom — after all, the stone itself is only temporary — then you will begin to see all walls only as temporary difficulties, waiting for someone else to come along and turn them into rubble.

Chapter Seven
What Do We Really Want To Do?

Let's be honest — most of us don't know what we want to do with our lives. We simply follow the pattern that society has laid out for us: study hard, go to college, get a job that will enable you to live comfortably, raise a family, and grow old happy. These are the steps we're given to follow, and by them, we are told, we will find fulfillment.

However, how many of us don't question if this really represents what we want at all?

The truth is that many of us simply run along on automatic pilot because that's what is expected. It is, after all, much easier than facing the uncertainty of having to make our own way. But stop and think seriously for a moment:

If nobody was telling you what to do — if there were no societal pressures or set ideas about success — what sort of life would actually make you happy? What would you do with your time? Would you pursue something entirely different from what society has conditioned us to believe is the right path?

Look beyond money, power, and what looks good at a cocktail party. These are all distractions, for they are not what really makes us feel alive.

The real question is — what brings you joy? What makes the blood flow through your veins, jazzes up your internal life, and starts an untold swarm of new possibilities, shifting and evolving in unexpected ways? What is something you could do for hours and never feel tired of at all?

It doesn't have to be some grand, world-transforming passion. Sometimes the minor things — the moments of simplicity — are what count most, whether it is writing, creating art, teaching, cooking, helping others, or just being in nature.

The point is that these little moments of joy can often be more significant than the larger, more conventional milestones society tells us to chase after.

Take a moment to reflect. Can you remember when was the last time you felt alive? When did you do something that made all thoughts of everything else disappear — except those of immeasurable beauty?

It may have been a talk with a good friend, walking alone in the woods, some work you did simply because doing it brought joy, or a time when you forgot the hours.

We frequently overlook these experiences in search of what we think we ought to want, but they give clues about what really matters to us.

If you don't know the answer yet, that's okay. Discovering your true desires is not something that happens overnight, and it can feel very frustrating at times.

But the key is to pay attention. All the things you like, all the things you are curious about, all the things that make you feel "plugged in" — this points toward the answer.

You may find that your passions change over time, and that's okay too. What matters is that you give yourself permission to explore, try new things, and hear the tiny sparks of interest that arise.

Life is filled with so many distractions, but if we learn to slow down a bit and pay attention to what makes us happy, then we will be able to see the necessary answer appear.

Challenge: Find Your Spark

Try the activities that give you the most joy for one week. This isn't about the things you "have" to do, but moments that truly feel like enjoyment or fulfillment.

Pay attention to how your body feels during these activities — does your heart beat faster? Do you find yourself smiling without even realizing it? Do you forget the time?

Look for patterns. What do these moments have in common? Are they all about creativity, learning, connection?

The point here isn't to judge or force any answers but to start becoming more aware of the things that truly light you up.

This exercise will give you incredible insight into what your soul truly wants. And once you begin to recognize patterns, each intentional step you take will lead you toward the things that bring you joy — guiding you to live a life filled with greater authenticity and fulfillment.

Chapter Eight
Playing the Man

Some folks play life like it's a chess game. They believe that as long as they obey the rules and make rational moves, they will win. There's nothing wrong with a good chess strategy, mind you. But let's be honest — life doesn't often break down that clearly.

The real winners? They're not just playing the game — they're playing the people.

As Harvey Specter says, *"Don't play the odds, play the man."*

Simply put, focus on behavior, not the condition. There's more to getting ahead in this game than "push this pawn here"; you need a sense of who your opponents are and what moves they might make against you. It's about changing other people's frames of mind for your own sake.

Once you know why others think what they do, want what they do, and act as they do — and once the answers are as black and white and simple as this — you'll see how you get to take your turn in the game of life. And once you start to understand these things, you don't have to follow the rules — you write your own rules.

At school: The smart student doesn't win every time. That often goes to the one who knows the system, who builds relationships and wins the right people's favor. Well, brains count, but the elevations in a classroom are not just based on good marks. It's about being seen as a figure of authority, someone who understands what is happening in classrooms and can use that knowledge to position oneself. It's about aligning your strengths with the right opportunities, and that often requires getting the rules of environments that never get written down.

At work: Succeeding means not just knowledge, but knowing office politics, power dynamics, and wisdom in action. Just being hard-working doesn't make you successful. You might be the hardest-working person in the room, but if you don't grasp the unwritten office rules, you could lose out on important opportunities.

Power dynamics exist everywhere: between peers, between headquarters and the field, between leaders and followers, and even within yourself, as your ambition conflicts with your personal growth.

Learning how to read the room and make strategic alliances, or how to project yourself effectively, can be a game-changer for climbing the ladder. Success is having the ability to know what is going on around you, how to act on it, and then acting on it before anyone else does.

In life: Success comes from knowing what people want, how they think, and how to get them to make the next move. Being the best isn't enough. Life is about random connections — a web that links everything and everyone. In social functions, business interactions, or relationships, the best results are determined by knowing what makes people tick.

The key is listening carefully, observing others' behaviors, and anticipating their needs before they even realize them. It's not manipulation — it's awareness.

It's not manipulation; it's enlightenment. Nobody can help advance your position in life more than someone who understands people, fears, desires, and motivations better than you do. Life is full of surprises, and even the best intentions might lead to disaster. But once you become an expert at reading people and finding out what drives them, when it comes to what they do, you don't need that many answers.

The only things you need are good instincts and timing. This kind of awareness allows you to stay one or two steps ahead, aware not only of what your next steps will be but how those around you may respond.

It's not necessarily who is the cleverest or works the hardest that really counts; it's about understanding the mood of those around you and being aware of the environment you live in.

You might find yourself in a situation where you can't see clearly ahead or do not have all the relevant facts at hand. At these times, beyond all else, trust your instincts. Knowing when to speak, when to listen, and when to act can often determine your success in life.

Life doesn't follow a simple script; it's more like improvisation. And if you can read the scene and the players, then you will always be able to act with confidence.

Exercise: Observe & Adapt

In your next interaction, try to operate actively. Not only listen to what the other person says, but also take in the non-verbal signs given off — body movement, gestures, looks. Those kinds of things can always tell us more than words do.

You might guess that this person is observant and understands what's going on beneath the surface, even if they don't say it directly. What does he really think of the topic being discussed? Are there unmentionable desires or fears that are subconsciously agitating him?

Make notes and analyze how the focus moves from all starring attention on what is said to these delicate signals.

Notice how doing this increases your empathy for the person as well as your grasp of their true point of view. At once, form a good habit. The rest of your life will surely benefit.

Chapter Nine
Nobody Cares

Life is wild. It doesn't stop for you. It doesn't slow down when things get hard, and it sure as hell doesn't wait until you get your act together.

And the truth? Most people don't care.

No time — they are all too busy wrestling with their own problems, running to stay alive instead of going beyond that, or dealing with their own concerns to take any interest in you.

That sounds extreme, but it's liberating when you get it.

For the most part, we are busy worrying about what others think of us, chasing after validation from someone else, and trying to find someone — anyone — to tell us it's okay if we're stuck in a rut (the things we don't like about ourselves).

We want someone to say, *"It's all right even though you don't fit the mold,"* or *"It's fine that you are not where you thought you'd be."*

In the grand scheme of things, everybody has enough trouble with their own messes to bother about fixing yours. And in fact, most people couldn't care less.

Your problems are not nearly so bothersome as you think they are to other folks.

When this realization hits, it feels like a revelation — liberating, with a feeling of nearly being relieved of a great weight upon your shoulders.

So much of our time is spent feeling like we have to be perfect, that we must live up to certain expectations, or get everything right before we dare let ourselves move forward at all.

But nobody is expecting us to get our act together.

Life still goes on, and it moves whether we get ready for it or not.

Everywhere you turn — no one cares.

It was like Sonny said in *A Bronx Tale*: **"Nobody cares."**

Did you not get the job? **No one cares.**

Failed the test? **No one cares.**

You lose your direction? **Nobody cares either.**

But this is actually nothing sad — it's freeing.

The minute you comprehend that the world is not going to sit on freeze for you to get your act together, that is when life begins to get interesting.

Author's Note

I used to overthink every interaction I had, convinced people were judging me for every word or gesture. I'd avoid situations where I had to meet new people because I was so afraid of making a mistake.

But one day, I forced myself to join a group discussion at work, even though my stomach was in knots. I stumbled over a few words, but instead of feeling embarrassed, I realized that no one cared as much as I thought.

The more I stopped worrying about being judged, the more I felt at ease, and the less anxiety I had.

It was like lifting a weight off my shoulders, knowing that I could be myself without needing everyone's approval.

***

You find that waiting for permission, for acknowledgment, for things to be just right is like running in circles.

No one is out there holding a green flag for you.

When you come to grips with this truth, two things happen:

- You stop endlessly waiting.
- You stop thinking of excuses.

You no longer believe that the world will give you a little more time — or somehow line up everything perfectly for you. And in that instant, you begin to live.

You start engaging in your own life.

You stop feeling the need to be judged.

You begin to rely on your own instincts, passions, and rhythms.

Life can be difficult to keep up with when everything is going so fast — but once you stop wanting it to ease down for you, you realize that you can pick the path that best suits you.

You can follow your own rhythm.

When you stop worrying as much about what others think of you, you gain the freedom to walk your own path.

You stop trying to be cast into the molds that other people have laid down for you, and you start to make your own.

**

We have this crazy idea that everyone is looking at us, judging us, and waiting for us to fall. But the truth is, people are more often concerned with their own lives than we realize.

They're not constantly watching our every move.

And once we grasp this, we have the freedom to move as we wish — without fearing the opinions of others.

It feels good.

You can take risks, make mistakes, and be honest without worrying about others waiting for an apology.

The power comes when we take the reins of our lives.

Live generously!

Don't need anyone's permission, you know?

Your life, your choices, your moves.

So long as you're not causing harm to others, by all means — be loud, be bold, be imperfect.

The millisecond you realize that nobody actually cares about your mistakes or your struggles, it frees you from fear and self-doubt.

And that is an extremely liberating feeling.

Challenge: Make a Bold Move

Do one thing you've felt too afraid to do for fear of what others would think.

It could be as simple as starting a conversation with someone you've admired from afar, wearing clothes that express your unique personality, or making choices that run against the tide.

Think about the experience after you've done it:

- Did it feel freeing?
- How much pressure were you really feeling?
- Did the world end because you did something out of the ordinary?

Taking this step will help you release that grip on perfection and rejection, and will open doors for your self-authenticity to shine through.

Chapter Ten
The Most of It

Why are we wasting our time on things that don't matter? Why do we waste our time and energy on these small things?

It's so easy to get caught up in the day-to-day — those petty arguments and minor frustrations that seem so urgent in any given moment. Fighting with your partner about who was responsible for putting the trash out, or complaining that someone took your parking spot.

Now, and I don't want to sound overly inspirational, but how many times have we let something so small, something so minuscule in the grand story of our lives, dig into us?

Was it really worth it after all?

Next time, pause. Take a breath, and ask yourself honestly: *"How long, really, is this problem going to last? Is it worth my time and energy? Is it worth fighting about?"*

If the answer is no, then simply let it go.

Let those little things go gently, with no drama. When you can't afford to waste time on anything irrelevant, you won't. Just consider how many days we spend wasting our time and energy worrying about things that don't matter in the grand scheme of things.

The curse of making a careless comment and having to deal with the cleanup. Holding your breath after hitting send on a text message or email.

Falling so deeply into an argument over something trivial that we lose precious time in our day.

Why do we torture ourselves like this? Why do we credit so much power to things that shouldn't have any?

These small, transitory moments steal our peace, taking us away from what actually matters.

Life doesn't stop when we're working through these tedious things. It continues with or without you, whether you care about it or not. So why not indulge while you still can?

What's the point of going round in circles, overthinking stuff?

Let go of the small things consciously, and make room for what truly nourishes you.

YOLO!

I rejoice in the ability to boogie down with people I don't know at a Tribute Doors show. Why? Because I've been afforded this opportunity, and life is short. Every moment we have to experience is a gift, and if we use that moment to second-guess or hold back, we miss out.

That impromptu, chaotic, happy stuff is what we remember. You only live once, and that's a limited time to make those memories count.

It's one of those sayings that people casually toss around without much thought. But when you actually think about it, isn't that the most simple and truest reminder of how to live your life?

It doesn't mean acting carelessly or irresponsibly when you are able to. It is challenging yourself, getting out of your comfort zone, taking chances, and saying **"yes!"** to the new opportunities instead of being restrained by fear or hesitancy.

Because in the end, those moments when you jumped, those are the moments you'll remember.

So what if you embarrass yourself? Who cares if it seems odd or wrong?

The fear of taking a risk is nothing compared to the regret of never trying. At the end of your life, you won't remember the times you played it safe. You'll remember those wild moments, those exhilarating moments, when you took a leap without knowing how you would land or didn't care how you would land.

You'll remember those moments when you overcame your fears, embraced adventure, and wound up in places you never thought you'd go.

That's what I want to always have in my life: fun, ridiculous, crazy memories that I can look back on and be like, *"Yeah, I really did that."*

Because when it's all said and done, that's all we really have all along. Memories.

Memories are what remain. However, matter and how you live in the moment are the only things in life. They are the things that make up who we are, the things that will stick with us long after the material possessions have come and gone.

Those aren't the right conditions to refine your skills.

Make today the moment. It is not tomorrow, not next year. The time to act is now. The time to live is today.

Exercise: The YOLO List

Make a list of 10 things you have striven to do but never done. These can be large or small — things that make your heart race with excitement, things you've always kept pushed to the side because of fear, doubt, or the limits you imposed on yourself.

When your list is complete, choose one item on that list and make a plan to do it in the next month. It doesn't matter how small or big the task is — what matters is that you go beyond your current comfort zone and actually do something.

You only get one shot at life, so create that memory now.

YOLO List

Chapter Eleven
Your Surroundings Are Everything

Ever been in the same vicinity as a person who, like, drains all energy and joy from the room? You know, the kind of person who walks into a room and the energy just feels heavier the moment they arrive? It's like you can sense the air thicken.

And then there are people who lighten the whole thing up — as in, you actually want to do something with your life, be inspired, get with it.

That's no accident. The people you keep around you are more important than you think.

You are the company you keep. The people around you affect your energy, your thoughts, your whole perspective on life. If you hang around negative people, you'll be pulled down into their negativity. Let go of the toxic energy and people who drain you, and make room for the ones who refill you.

And I don't mean just toxic people in the most obvious way — the manipulators or liars or people who pull you into pointless drama. Yes, those people need to go. But there's also a quiet toxic approach that can be even trickier to detect.

They are the ones who never applaud your successes, who challenge your ideas, who cause you to feel small, doubt yourself, or make you feel bad about yourself every single day. These are the people whose circle you should not join.

Consider the relationships that seem one-sided — the ones in which you always give and never seem to receive. Those are the people you want to shut out.

You deserve people in your life who vibe at your level, who support you when you're struggling, not just root for you when you're winning.

The ones who only check in when you're winning and disappear when you enter a rough patch? They're not your friends. They're viewers.

They're waiting like it's a reality show — sitting at home, waiting for a juicy episode to come on so they can watch from the comfort of their own lives, and only when it's convenient for them.

But here's the thing: it's not always so simple to remove toxic people. Sometimes they're people you've known your entire life — people you grew up with, loved ones, a former crush. And that's what makes it so complicated.

If someone's been in your life that long, it's easy to rationalize their behavior.

"That's just how they are."

"They don't mean any harm."

"Maybe I'm overreacting."

But here's the hard truth: **you're not overreacting**. If a person is dragging you down, taking your energy away, or letting negativity affect every part of your life, it's not your responsibility to fix them.

Authors Note

When I was younger, I had a friend who seemed fun at first. We'd laugh together, joke around, and have a good time. But looking back, I can see how much negativity he brought into my life. He spread rumors about me and got me into trouble, all because I was too gullible to see it at the time.

He would only show me true kindness every so often, and I mistook that for friendship. But deep down, I knew I wasn't being treated the way I deserved.

It wasn't easy to let him go, especially since we'd shared so many laughs. But eventually, I realized I had a circle of friends who actually treated me better and made me feel valued.

It's hard to let go of people you've been close to, but sometimes, you have to choose the ones who truly support you over those who drain your energy.

Your Responsibility is to Guard Your Peace

Energy is contagious. The people you spend time with influence your thinking, your behavior, and your perspective — whether you're aware of it or not.

If you're around people all the time who moan, complain, or constantly highlight the negative aspects of life — guess what? You'll begin to see the world in the same way.

You Will Become the Same as the Energy You Are Surrounded By

But if you hang around successful, risk-taking, big-thinkers, you will pick up their mindset, too. You're going to be more ambitious, more daring, more willing to take risks.

You are a product of your environment — good or bad.

But this is not only about the people around you. You don't even see how much your environment affects you, too.

The books you read, the TV shows you binge, the social media accounts you follow — everything you consume is programming your brain, whether you realize it or not.

That's the energy you're putting out into the world.

If the only things you're putting into your mind are negativity or drama, that's the energy you're giving out into the world. You'll be put in a position where you adopt that same toxic mindset.

But when you expose yourself to things that push you, inspire you, challenge your thinking, and provoke growth, you'll start to see your own perspective shift.

This creates a new mental space as you choose to surround yourself with positivity, inspiration, and growth.

Step back and give it some real thought.

Is your environment pushing you forward or pulling you back? Are the people in your life helping you, or weighing you down?

If it is the latter, **change it**. You **can** change that.

Cut out the noise. Be with those who raise your own levels — those who push you to be a better you.

Set up your environment to favor who you want to be — a space in your body and mind that welcomes your success, growth, and transformation.

And here's the thing: if you want to step up in life, it all begins with making sure you've got the right environment.

If you aren't in the right environment — the people, the place, and the state of mind — you're stuck in a pattern, asking yourself why nothing ever changes.

The reality is that transformation begins with what you expose yourself to.

Choose wisely. You have to create the life you want, beginning with the space you occupy internally and externally.

Challenge: Audit Your Circle

Take a moment to reflect. List the five people you spend the most time with.

Do they uplift or drain you?

Do they inspire your growth, or do they bind you?

Once you have this list, run your mental eye over each of them and ask yourself:

- *Are they leading you to success?*
- *Do they inspire positive energy?*

If any of these people are draining you or adding to your negativity, consider what you can do to change it — even in small ways.

What can you do to limit their influence in your life? Establish boundaries or distance if needed from people who are not helping you grow anymore.

You should be surrounded by people who bring out the best in you.

Evaluate Your Inner Circle

_____

_____

_____

_____

_____

_____

_____

_____

Chapter Twelve
Fear of Giving Up

Letting go is one of the more liberating experiences we can have as humans — and one of the most difficult. The concept of relinquishing control feels deeply unnatural, particularly when what we're clinging to has a hue of the familiar — even if that isn't in our best interest. Human nature is such that we cling to what we know and are comfortable with, and this feels safe and stable. But over the years, what once brought us contentment eventually becomes a burden, preventing growth and change.

We hold on to the familiar because the unknown is uncertain, risky, and full of potential failure. It's much easier to remain in a situation — even if it's not great — than to take a chance and enter into the unknown, where we have no idea what the outcome will be. This fear of change is simply a natural instinct to avoid discomfort. The unknown potentially involves pain, disappointment, or failure, and many of us don't want to face those prospects. The known might not be ideal, but it's more secure.

The society we live in has conditioned us to feel that stability is success and uncertainty is disorder. We are conditioned to think that the more gratitude we have, the more we control. And further, the more we have, the greater they become — in both material and social aspects.

And so many of us remain stuck in situations — in jobs we despise, relationships that drain us, or beliefs that no longer align with our reality. The pain of the known is better than the fear of the unknown. Which means we go on, we pretend, and we cling to familiarity, silently hoping, in ways we don't even express, that things will somehow work themselves out.

But what if we're wrong?

What if the secret to success is not to hold on, but to let go?

Because maybe the thing that scares us the most — the act of letting go — is precisely the thing that will set us loose. When we stay attached to what is known, we close the door to growth. We prevent ourselves from evolving and ever becoming who we are meant to be. While we may feel comfortable in our habits, we may limit ourselves from reaching our best selves.

This fear of letting go isn't just about loss — the people or things we'll no longer have — but also about change, an uncertain future, and, at its core, the fear that without them, we might not be enough. We define ourselves by what we do, the relationships we have, and what we own. Having to let go of these feels like letting go of a part of ourselves. We're scared that if we shed what we know, we will lose our sense of identity, or we won't be able to recreate things from scratch.

Why Some People Fear Change

As we are insecure, we are afraid of letting go. Or we fear that letting go of the familiar will reveal us to the world as incapable, inadequate, or unworthy. These fears almost never turn out to be true, but they are hardwired into our brains. We've been trained to believe that our worth is tied to our achievements, what we own, and our relationships in society. If all these external markers of success disappeared, who would we truly be?

This is the conditioning of our society. From an early age, we are taught that success is defined by what we have, what we achieve, and how we compare to others. And with that, success becomes inseparably tied to our sense of self-worth. What we are really afraid of is that we will not be seen as successful when we stop. And without that measurement of success, we become invisible and unimportant and insignificant.

In a world where those around us — friends, family, relatives — still praise and validate us for our external achievements and lavish lifestyles, it becomes difficult to let go, as our identity is deeply intertwined with them.

But without all these things, who are we?

Who are we really, underneath the job title, the stuff, and the social status?

This is the key question we should be asking ourselves. Letting go of external attachments allows us to reconnect with our true selves, free from society's labels.

In a way, this is like a tree dropping its leaves in autumn. It is not afraid to lose them because it understands that this is needed for new growth. The process of releasing the things, people, and beliefs that do not serve us allows for new growth, new experiences, and new opportunities.

Letting go makes room for growth. Just like a tree doesn't mourn its lost leaves but embraces the new season, we should welcome change and what's to come.

The "What's the Worst That Could Happen?" Challenge

One solution for fear of letting go is to confront it head on. And this is because one form of hope starts by recasting the scenario of the worst possible outcome.

We blow up the fear of what might happen to be something way bigger than it actually is. But as we use logic to challenge our most wicked fears, we learn even in the worst of worst-case scenarios, we will be okay.

The fear starts to lose its grip on us.

What will the worst be if you let go of this situation?

Write it down. Now, ask yourself:

- What's the absolute worst that can happen here?
- This is just one of a million things that could happen.
- What if this came to pass — what would I do? Could I handle it?
- If I survived, what would I learn from this experience?

This is not an activity to discount your feelings, but rather to acknowledge them with a sense of calm presence and logic.

Reflection

_____

_____

_____

_____

_____

_____

_____

_____

You'll see that when we're clearer about the consequences, we realize
we've always been stronger and more resilient than we knew.

Chapter Thirteen
The Delusion of Success

As for success, most of us follow someone else's definition. This hand we have been dealt, a script we read, an outline of what makes each of us successful in society.

The script is that we go to school, get a good job, have a house, settle down, save for retirement, and eventually achieve the "American Dream" (or whatever that is in my case) in one form or another. But is that the road to happiness? Or maybe it's just a conveyor belt we're all placed on, moving us through life without ever really pausing to think about what we want from it.

Success: A Personal Choice or External Indicators

What if it's not about getting X, Y, Z, but instead, doing what's true to us? What if the ultimate formula for success isn't how much wealth you've amassed or the material items you acquire, but rather peace, fulfillment, and purpose in the life you create?

It Is All a Myth of "Success" — How to Unbind

In so many ways, the modern world tries to impose a single definition of success. It's an expectation that people everywhere are expected to follow, and those who don't are often labeled as losers.

But the truth is, success is a very personal thing. It's about what lights you up, what makes you feel completely alive, what reflects your true self.

It's being called into question by more and more people along the conventional success-hustler-safety-net-corporate-ladder route. Entrepreneurs, artists, and free spirits are leaving traditional jobs and structures behind to pursue alternative lifestyles. These lifestyles may not promise fame or fortune, but they often lead to a deep sense of well-being.

Our Training on Reframing Success on Your Own Terms

And on that note, you have to live a successful life — but it has to be *your* vision of that. It means removing yourself from everything and everyone suggesting how you ought to live, and instead, living your life on your terms.

Success is not about comparing yourself to your peers or pursuing social validation — it is about constructing a life that feels authentic to who you are.

Exercise: Redefine Success on Your Own Terms

Stop and consider what success looks like for you. What does your dream life look like, free from the influence of society?

Write down the following:

- What kind of day would be a win for you?
- And you know, what would the mirror of your relationships look like when success means love, connection, joy — not status?
- What would you do if success was about fulfillment, not achievement?

This will help you develop a vision of what success looks like for you — one that is rooted in your own values, not someone else's plan.

Reflection

_____

_____

_____

_____

_____

_____

_____

_____

To Free Oneself from Conditioned Thinking

It is one of the most freeing things that we can do — unlearning these limiting beliefs and beginning to question everything we have been taught.

What if all the lies we were programmed to believe about money, success, relationships, and happiness were actually working against us? And what if the real answer is somewhere else?

Unlearning is, therefore, uncomfortable — even painful — because it requires us to dismantle the very foundation on which we've built our understanding of the world. But it is also one of the most freeing experiences we can have. In exploring beliefs that no longer serve us, we break the chains of conditioning that have kept us prisoners of a life we never asked for.

The Power of Self-Inquiry

Self-inquiry — questioning everything we think we know — is the secret to unlearning. We must step back and see our beliefs with a critical eye.

This isn't about burning the bridge before crossing it, but about carefully choosing which paths truly serve us in the present.

The Self-Inquiry Journal: Physical Activity

Spend a few minutes writing out five beliefs you have about your life. These can also be beliefs about love, money, your career, and the things that have shaped your worldview. Then, ask yourself:

- What leads to such a belief?
- Is it true?
- How does this belief shape my life?

- Am I serving myself well or not?
- What would it look like to let go of that belief?

Reflection

_____

_____

_____

_____

_____

_____

_____

This process, practiced regularly, allows you to shed the layers of conditioning that no longer serve you, creating space for thoughts and beliefs that inspire and empower you.

Chapter Fourteen
Nature Is The Best Teacher

Natural beauty is something humans tend to take for granted. It flows without question, with faith in the rhythms and cycles that existed long before we ever did. As Karen Maezen Miller once said:

"A river doesn't ask whether it should keep flowing."

A tree never asks where it should grow. A wolf knows nothing about living the "right" life. They are attuned to themselves and their surroundings, trusting instinct, allowing life's cadence to unfold without a fight.

The balance of nature is something that can easily be forgotten by humans. We are always seeking something beyond today, chasing the next big thing, questioning what we have, doubting the choices we made. In nature, though, no such inner battle exists. No second-guessing or overthinking. It simply exists.

As human beings, it is our blessed gift to self-realize — to see the world through our own intentions rather than through others. And yet, all too often, this awareness is our worst enemy. We want to question, doubt, and second-guess ourselves. We overthink every decision, loathe every potential outcome, and dread every unknown.

But instead of surrendering, we resist, cling, and hold onto the illusion of control. Meanwhile, nature simply is. It doesn't reflect on its own conduct, nor does it seek to micromanage its fate. It just goes on, unburdened by the need to conform to a preconceived template.

By doing this, we have brought forth systems and structures that govern our lives in exchange for innate knowledge about how we naturally understand the world. Our culture conditions us to quantify success in terms of tangible goods: money, status, accomplishment. But nature tells us success isn't always something to hold. It is a process of being. It is a continuation, a flow. The key, ironically, is not what we cling to.

Living like a River

The movement of a river teaches important lessons about life. A river never fights with the landscape; it adjusts, even reshaping the land if it must. It doesn't try to cling to past versions of itself — upstream it was one thing, downstream it is another. It moves forward, as is its way. There is no resistance, only flow.

The river does not travel in a straight line, or in any direction you can predict. It snakes and spirals, sometimes quickly, sometimes slowly, sometimes violently, and other times softly. And it always streams ahead, welcoming every shift in direction without criticism. It does not question the barriers it faces; it only wants a way to navigate around them.

Here, a river reminds us that we don't have to challenge the things that come up in life. We don't have to resist the inevitable shifts that come. The only option left is to learn how to trust that there always exists a way out, even when we cannot see it.

Imagine if we lived our life the way a river flows. What if we didn't fight the obstacles we faced, but instead looked for ways to move through or around them? What if, instead of clinging to the illusion of permanence, we learned to welcome movement and change as a fact of life?

A river has no fear of the road ahead of it; it relies on its course. Similarly, we could discover that trusting the unfolding of life, rather than reaching to control it, brings much greater happiness and peace.

The fear of leaving the bubble of what we know makes it a prison. We hold on to what we know because there is comfort in that familiarity, but that familiar ground is stagnant ground. We must shake off the chains of complacency and comfort in order to unlock our true potential.

It's not always easy to let go, particularly in a world that trains us to think we should be in control all the time. But it is incredibly freeing to learn to let go and go with the natural flow of life.

The more we resist the inevitable transformations that life brings, the more we suffer. But when we release — when we surrender to the current carrying us — we align with something larger than just our own fears. The ride becomes smoother. Opportunities arrive as if by design. We know when to act and when to sit back and let things play out in the right order. We listen to the music of life itself.

Exercise: The River Visualization

To really internalize this lesson, find a place where you can sit without being interrupted.

[CLOSE YOUR EYES, BREATHE, IMAGINE YOU'RE A RIVER.]

Imagine the terrains you drift through — twisting woods, open expanses, steep valleys. Imagine the times that the path gets blocked: fallen trees, jagged rocks, wrong turns.

How does the river respond? Do you come to a halt and panic or resist?

No.

It finds a way forward. It travels under, over, or around whatever blocks its path.

Now apply this image to your own life. What problems are you dealing with? Where have you been swimming upstream?

Can you envision a scenario in which you are just where you need to be — where every twist, turn, knot, and bend is part of you being written, you being created?

Stop fighting the stream. Surrender to let it pull you ahead, and allow yourself to feel how effortless things become as a result of that surrender.

Think about how common it is to hold onto things or people who no longer serve us. Be it an old habit, an unhealthy relationship, or work that doesn't satisfy us, we hesitate to change because we fear what lies ahead.

However, as the river flows, so too must we — *embrace change*. You have to let go in order to make room for things you didn't even think about.

The earth is shaped in the wake of the river as it carves its way through the land. And by letting go, we open up new paths to our future that we don't even have language for right now.

Let go of control, and trust that in surrendering to the flow of life, we just might end up where we need to be — more in alignment with who we really are.

***

The only way we can start to live in trust, surrender, and peace is to learn from the wild.

Nature does not tarry, and so should we not.

We must let go of the need to control, trust the process, and flow with life unfolding.

We do this to align ourselves with the natural rhythms of the world and to make our journey more peaceful.

Chapter Fifteen
Minimalism and Freedom

In a society that bombards us with messages on how to consume more — things and status, both thrilling experiences and bitter — we might be left with the feeling that we are endlessly pursuing something we don't fully understand. In a world of abundance, the phrase *"less is more"* genuinely applies.

The more we have — possessions, responsibilities, obligations — the more our lives become a weight. When we believe, *"Once I achieve this/move to this place/marry this person, I will be comfortable, secure, happy,"* it becomes clutter — clutter in our homes, our minds, our relationships, our calendars. We constantly take on more space, more stuff, more distractions, as if that will fulfill some sense of incompleteness we feel inside us. But in reality, we just become heavier.

We've created lives loaded with things we don't want — trinkets, gadgets, appointments, obligations — and the overall weight of all this makes us feel stuck. The things we wanted to own somehow end up owning us. *More* has become an endless pursuit, a futile cycle of promises that delivers nothing.

What if, instead of filling every moment with activity and every space with clutter, we were blessed with the gift of simplicity? What if we could strip away distraction and excess, and get back to only what speaks to the heart?

Minimalism isn't simply about dividing with the clutter we own — it's about dividing with life. It's about eliminating the noise and excess that cloud our sight and making room for clarity, meaning, and presence.

The Freedom of the Art of Letting Go

Minimalism is a practice that encourages us to pull back and ask ourselves: *What is truly valuable in my life?*

In a culture that constantly bombards us with a message of *"more, more, more"* — more stuff, more accomplishments, more experiences — it takes a lot of courage to stand your ground and say, *Enough.*

We are always in a state of motion, gathering, achieving, but we often feel emptier afterward than we did before. The more we have, the more difficult it is to cope. When we release what is not necessary, what is not serving our purpose, we no longer feel the need to keep up, to have what others have, or to prove ourselves through material possessions.

Somewhere between acceptance and letting go is the ability to trust. We begin to believe we don't need more to be happy. We believe our worth is not measured in our possessions or a laundry list of accomplishments. The only wealth is also the only true wealth — not "stuff," but the fullness of experience and relationship; the fullness of connection to ourselves, others, and all that matters.

Living a simplified life doesn't mean sacrificing joy or abundance — it means getting in alignment with what's most important and saying no to everything else. That includes the things you leave behind: all the meaningless clutter, the relationships that drain you, and the commitments that don't align with your true self.

Author's Note

I used to be in a relationship that appeared to be perfect at the beginning, but which gradually turned into a toxic routine.

She was kind, and in the beginning, everything seemed fine. But over time, I noticed that it was starting to have an effect on me. She would make me feel bad, belittle me, and then only listen to me long enough to tell me I was wrong — and then repeat that I never listened.

I felt like I was tiptoeing around her all the time, trying to keep the peace, keep her happy — and nothing I did was enough. It was getting old, and I was losing myself. I had ignored all the red flags for far too long, telling myself they'd all get better if only I tried harder.

Finally, I'd had enough.

I realized I couldn't continue to pour so much of myself into a person who didn't appreciate or respect me. It was difficult to leave, but it was the only way I could begin to heal and regain control of my life. It took me a while to trust myself again, to be confident again, but I knew I deserved to be in a relationship where I could thrive — and not just simply survive.

***

Imagine a life where your schedule is shaped by your values, not by the pressure to perform or the desire to please. A full life — not because of what you have, but because of how fully you embrace what remains.

Minimalism is not about lacking; it's about living with intention. It's about crafting a life that captures who you really are, and not what society thinks should matter to you. There's a lot less focus on how much you own, and more on how you interact with what you do have — your time, energy, space, and relationships.

The Peace of Simplifying

When we let go of the unnecessary, we create space for peace. We make room for what's most vital in our lives — our health, our relationships, our passions, and our sense of self.

It is here — where the real freedom lies — through the act of letting go. We live in an age and culture where there is tremendous pressure to gain, to demonstrate, to get ahead. However, by learning to detach ourselves from these external markers, we liberate ourselves from the chains of expectations.

We discover that we are enough just as we are, without all the things we believed we needed.

Letting go isn't always easy. It forces us to interrogate how attached we are to things and to confront the fear that, if we release what we have, we'll end up with less. But the truth is that when we let go of the clutter, we've also freed ourselves — and gained something so much more: **freedom**.

We liberate ourselves from the relentlessness of *more*, and in that liberation, we discover we indeed have *enough*. We make room to experience life more fully and authentically.

The Subtraction Method Exercise

To embrace minimalism, start with this simple exercise:

Choose one thing in each of the three pillars of your life that no longer adds value:

- An object that you're no longer using or requires you.
- A duty or responsibility that depletes you rather than energizes you.
- Something that you were willing to leave — but had to mentally leave first.

Let go of them — donate or discard the item, step away from the commitment, challenge the belief.

Think about how you feel after doing this. Do you feel lighter? More at ease? Free from the load of all that you owned?

If you let go of what you don't need every time, you make room for what you do. As time goes on, this practice becomes a muscle you build. When you let go of physical clutter, mental clutter, and emotional clutter, you gain clarity, freedom, and a deeper peace.

Chapter Sixteen
Rebellions and Authenticity

Rebellion equals freedom for a lot of people. So, they think the height of independence is rejecting norms, questioning authority, or going against social expectations. No wonder rebellion seems like the way to assert our individuality and be free of constraints. We believe we are paving our own way by swimming upstream.

But rebellion, at its heart, is a reaction — it's a response to something outside oneself, not an intentional act of creation.

True freedom isn't found in rebelling against everything the world presents to you. It's not about refusing things solely for the sake of making a point. Real freedom is about knowing what fits with who we truly are and what doesn't. Freedom is choosing a way to live rather than reacting to what others want.

Without limits, rebellion is a different cage — it is the hamster wheel of negativity. It's still being influenced from the outside, just pushing against the social order you're part of.

The Power of Authenticity

Intention differentiates between rebellion and authenticity. A rebel rejects social orders just because they exist, while an independent person evaluates them and chooses the ones that align with their true self.

Being authentic doesn't mean we need to throw out everything in our environment that doesn't feed us; it means we need to embrace what makes us feel good and let go of the rest.

Authenticity is not a statement — it's how we express our true selves, regardless of others' expectations.

When we choose to live authentically, we live as who we really are, even if it doesn't meet the standards of others. It's about taking the road less traveled, even if that road is rocky or untraveled, because we know it to be the only way to be genuine.

Authenticity isn't about defying others — it's about accepting yourself. It's about living from a place of truth, guided by our inner values — not because we want to fight the system, but because to do anything else is not being true to ourselves.

A genuine individual realizes that authenticity is about owning your values, not blaming your surrounding environment. Rebellion might be the first step on the early path toward freedom, but it is not the foundation on which freedom stands.

We often give up parts of ourselves to do what's right for others, but in those fleeting moments of self-awareness and acceptance, we find it in ourselves to do what we want — and what is right for us.

The path to authenticity isn't bold or noisy; it's a quiet rebellion — a return to who we've always been beneath society's pressures.

An Exercise in Living the Authentic Life

Identify a specific area of your life where you're far from your truth. This may come in the form of your work, relationships, or habits that you've built up over time. Pay attention to where your values are being undermined, or where you've subsumed your own to the expectations of other people in your life.

Write down the following:

- **Which expectation am I living up to?**
  This might be a societal norm, family tradition, or professional standard that you feel pressured to uphold.
- **Is this consistent with my true values, or is it forced?**
  Ask yourself if this expectation is aligned with your authentic self or if it feels pressed upon you.
- **What would you be doing differently if you were living authentically?**
  Consider how your decisions would be different if they were based on your genuine self instead of external pressure.

Now, pledge to make one move today that gets you closer to being the authentic you in this area. This could mean:

- Establishing a boundary with someone or something that depletes your energy.
- Declining an obligation that doesn't reflect your real wishes.
- Taking the first step toward something that really speaks to you — either a personal passion or a core value.

It could also be as simple as taking a moment to listen to yourself and honor what you really feel, even if it's different from what you were told you should feel.

Reflection

_____

_____

_____

_____

_____

_____

_____

In time, these baby steps will accumulate and become strides. Over time, you will stop resisting society's rules and begin living in harmony with your true self.

The more you behave authentically, the more authentic freedom you'll experience by being you.

Notice this: the impulse to rebel simply disappears when you cease to react to the world and start building your own life based upon your own truth.

Chapter Seventeen
The Beauty of Solitude

Solitude has a bad reputation these days — an emptiness to be filled, not a gift to be savored. Notifications, social media, and life clutter pull us in a million directions every day. We are taught to see a solitary life as lonely, and that silence should be avoided. We think we must constantly be doing something or be with someone.

But authentic solitude — the quiet, focused time we spend alone turning inward — is what fosters clarity, unlocks creativity, and reveals insights hidden beneath the noise and distractions of the external world.

When we are alone, we listen to ourselves. These rare moments of silence give us space to digest our experiences and reconnect with what truly matters. And if we don't allow room for quiet to happen, we leave ourselves open to the possibility of becoming lost. Without moments of space to think, life becomes a tangled mess.

Alone does not equal lonely — solitude is about psychological and emotional openness, making it possible for us to be more alive and engaged. It serves as a reminder to press the "pause" button and see life from a better place — a perspective uncluttered by the noise that so often distorts our thinking and distracts us from what we truly want.

The Beauty of Being Alone

Being alone is fine, as long as you don't feel lonely. There's only so much we can know about what others are thinking, and time by ourselves allows us to recharge, think, and strip away distractions to focus on our thoughts.

It's in these low times that we often discover new truths about ourselves, our destination, and what's important. Without outside distractions, we are free to explore our thoughts as honestly and deeply as we want. Moments like these challenge us to ask ourselves meaningful questions, free of outside opinions.

Solitude can be a sanctuary — a space where we can hear our thoughts clearly, without interruptions. It gives us more self-awareness, more independence, and teaches us how to enjoy our own company. We can be ourselves — alone, without others dictating our actions. We simply exist.

Even silence brings new insights, like unexplored paths in a peaceful forest. In those moments, we are reminded how liberating it can be — just to be — without society's voice whispering what we should be.

It brings us back to who we are when we spend time with only ourselves. We cut attachments to worldly distractions that cloud our grasp of who we are. Solitude helps us put our focus back on what we actually want and care about — what matters to us most.

Creating these moments allows us time and space to explore thoughts and ideas we may have buried during everyday life. This is a time to think about ourselves alone, without worldly distractions attempting to guide our goals.

Challenge: Solitude Experiment

Go spend a whole day all by yourself. Put your phone in the other room, shut your computer down, and do not go running for entertainment or outside approval. Just be with yourself.

Notice what thoughts and feelings come up when there's nothing to distract you. At first, diving into this experiment may feel scary, but it's a place for you to deepen your connection with yourself and discover elements of truth that have been out of your line of sight.

If your day is over, keep a journal throughout the day to reflect on your experience:

- What feelings emerged for you in your alone time? Did you feel at peace or uneasy?
- Did you have moments of calm, or did your mind wander to distractions?
- What did you learn about yourself when there wasn't external noise?
- How was this experience transformative in terms of your needs and desires?

Reflection

_____

_____

_____

_____

_____

_____

_____

_____

This exercise will show you that solitude is not something to fear, but a source of great strength. The better we get at being alone, the more we generate internal stability. This allows us to approach the world with more confidence and clarity, as we look less to outside opinions and more to our instincts.

Being alone gives us the opportunity to reflect on the deepest thoughts, feelings, and beliefs we have, and helps us to live more purposefully.

Being alone allows us to find out who we really are. It allows us to tune in to what we require and take back our mental and emotional space. The struggles that push for innovations ultimately lead to liberation.

Solitude gives us the time to be more intentional and authentic, letting our inner compass guide the way. The more we lean into our solitude, the more we stop seeing it as something to fear and instead recognize it as a tool for personal development — an opportunity to gather ourselves, reflect, and come out on the other end more self-aware than before.

Chapter Eighteen
The Courage to Walk Away

Living an authentic life requires the courage to shed anything you've outgrown, even if it looks good to others. Leaving behind a life that seems successful on the outside but feels wrong on the inside is one of the most difficult things to do.

Take, for example, Jack. He didn't have to give up his six-figure job in the city and walk away from the conventional "right" path that friends, family, and society advocated. Instead, Jack did something many would deem reckless — he walked away.

But it wasn't a decision he made rashly. It slowly became clear to Jack that the life he had built wasn't the one he wanted. He had spent years climbing the corporate ladder, collecting things, and pretending to be successful. But inside, he felt empty. His life appeared perfect on the outside, but such a life did not make him happy at all. He understood it wasn't his life; it was just the life he had fallen into.

So Jack made the leap. He gave up his luxury apartment, his six-figure job, and the city he had always known. His family and friends said he was making a terrible mistake, but Jack knew it was the right decision.

He was asked why, and he replied, *"It wasn't my life."*

Success as defined by other people meant nothing to him unless it was built on his own version of success.

The story of Jack reminds us that letting go of what doesn't serve us is a powerful act of courage. He wasn't after money or status; he was after freedom and truth. His story reminds us that sometimes, to get more in touch with the life we really want to live, we need to discard the things we thought we couldn't live without.

Jack's choice wasn't hasty; it was the result of years of self-discovery. He had worked desperately to build the life he believed he desired. But he eventually saw it wasn't really his. It had been molded by the expectations of others, stuffed with material possessions and achievements he didn't give a damn about. The wake-up call was realizing that his success had come at the cost of his happiness.

One day, Jack woke up and realized something: he wanted out — out of the beautiful apartment, the job nobody could ever complain about, the comfort, the stability. His family was shocked. His friends laughed at his decision, and his colleagues thought he was throwing away everything.

But Jack had something they didn't have: the life he was living wasn't actually his. He had been following someone else's dream and was now ready to follow his.

Jack's story is one of bravery and possibility. It demonstrates that we can all decide to walk away from a life we don't fit in. It takes honesty to admit our own dissatisfaction and bravery to turn aside the things we've been conditioned to desire. Each step Jack took away from his old life brought him closer to one far richer and more meaningful than any amount of money or fame could have given him.

It's the wild ones — those who refuse to follow a script — who teach us that real freedom isn't about what we own or what we have on our business cards. It's in how real we are living. They leave us with a most basic question:

"Am I really living my life, or am I just chasing someone else's dream?"

These bold stories make me question my own path. When are you living your truth, or someone else's? Being willing to let go of what no longer serves you can lead you to the authentic life that's truly yours — a colorful, bold, and adventurous life like those who dared to take the leap before you.

Chapter Nineteen
On Natural Living: A Practical Manual

Living naturally is not just something that happens as you wait; it is a conscious, waking choice you make each day. It's about having the freedom to be true, to live authentically, and to pursue progress. To live authentically is a challenge. It takes time, consciousness, and intention — every day — to remember that we do not have to conform in order to live. It's about unlearning things, relearning things, rediscovering the beauty of your desires, and dismantling the systems around you that keep you from fully living the life you want.

Reading about how to live authentically can be inspiring, but it's of little value if you don't put it into practice. The magic only happens when we live what we learn — when we apply the insights into our daily lives, from how we spend our time to the conversations we have and the choices we make. Living naturally is not just a thing of the mind, but a matter of living the truth in our bones.

Living from a wild heart means blazing your own trail and creating a life true to your best self. It's about resisting the pull of comfort and moving forward despite the unknown and the challenges. This isn't about being reckless or careless; it's about pursuing balance with your passions in life — where your fears, insecurities, and limitations don't pull the strings. Instead of dreading the unknown, we approach it not with fear but with curiosity — with a desire to learn, grow, and experience the world in its rawness.

93

For most people, it is fear that stands between them and living naturally — fear of failure, fear of being judged by people, fear of not knowing what might happen tomorrow. These are the chains that tie people down to the ground. Fear is just the ego's way of trying to save you from the pain of moving out of your place of familiarity. However, the truth is that change is part of nature and life, and if you want to live out your dreams, you have to be willing to speak up and step outside the line set for you by others.

Living naturally requires showing up with the courage to live out your inner self, no matter how weird it may sound.

Does it mean you have to run from your relationships and start a life on the streets all alone?

Of course not!

It just means it's time you started living by your standards. Most of the time, it's pushing to do whatever you love to your heart's desire. It means doing what makes you sleep soundly — because that's the only way you'll have smoother days.

Pick Something That's Been Sucking Your Soul

Take a few minutes to check out your life: where you've been spending most of your time and what sucks the life out of you. It could be your job, your house, a person around you, or a belief system you've been forced into living with for years. Take note of whatever has been making your life hell, and today, make a resolution to ditch it.

To live naturally often begins with having the bravery to see that something isn't working for you. It requires the honesty to recognize that change is needed, and then the will to bring that change about. It's about defying expectations, pushing boundaries, and refusing to let fear prohibit you from exploring.

Re-Discover What You Truly Want

The demands and expectations of other people are easy to get swept along with. Too often, we lose sight of what we want, buried under a mountain of "shoulds" and "musts." We live our lives under the expectations of family, friends, or society as a whole without ever checking to see if these expectations even resonate with us on a soul level.

Take a step back. Pause and ask yourself: *"What do I really want from life?"*

"What leaves me feeling alive, happy, engaged?"

"What would my dream day look like, without the pressure of anyone else's expectations?"

Take some time to reconnect with your own desires and passions, free from anyone else's influence. Give yourself permission to redefine what it means to truly live — on your own terms.

Such reflection needs stillness — space and time to reconnect with your center, away from the noise and distractions around you. In these quiet moments, we can listen to our hearts and respond to the call of our truest self.

Put Aside What Society Wants

As we age, we take on the expectations of the people around us — parents, teachers, media, society at large. We internalize these narratives over time until we start to think they are our own. We're told to try to fit into a certain mold, to pursue goals that aren't even ours. But after some time, there's a question we need to ask: *"Are these expectations truly my own?"*

In what areas of your life do you experience pressure to conform? Are the goals you're striving for really satisfying your needs? Or are you just pursuing someone else's dream?

Pick one expectation that doesn't serve you anymore — and liberate it. You may feel uneasy for a while, but over time, it will give you the freedom to create and maintain a life that truly belongs to you.

Make Life Easier

Natural living isn't simply about removing everything excess in your life; it's about simplifying everything too — physically, mentally, and emotionally. The stuff, the confusion, the distractions, and the demands of life overwhelm us, preventing us from living simply and finding clarity and focus. Minimalism isn't just about minimizing; it's about making room for what's most important.

Look around at your surroundings. What possessions do you have that no longer bring you joy? What relationships (even with family members) drag you down? What commitments weigh you down?

Start with small steps. Release one: in each part of your life, out it goes — an article of clothing, an obligation, even a belief or habit that's no longer getting you where you want to go.

96

When you remove these layers of excess, you can live more fully — with more intention and purpose.

Decluttering is not just a physical process; it is an act of deep symbolism. It's so important to invite the new into our lives, and the only way to do this is by releasing what does not work anymore. When you naturally live this way, you cut the noise and make way for clarity to go forth.

Rewrite: Blueprint for Wild Living

Now that you have a better idea of what it means to be natural, write out a plan for your untamed life. Begin by identifying the places in your life where you feel limited or suffocated. Then select one area and find an easy action step today that breaks you out. It can be something as simple as saying "no" to a commitment that you are no longer interested in, spending time in nature to reconnect with yourself, or starting a creative project that makes your heart sing.

Reflection

_____

_____

_____

_____

_____

_____

_____

_____

You can promise yourself to take bold steps toward living your truth —
and follow through. Small, consistent actions, day by day, will gradually lead
to bigger changes. Each step brings you closer to the life you want, with
progress — not perfection — being the key.

Chapter Twenty
Reflections and Challenges

We absorb the energy and influence of those around us. That doesn't mean we should broadcast every thought. Instead, real strength lies in discerning the good people in our lives from those who aren't.

The world — the external circumstances — doesn't give us true freedom. It's not something passed down to us or given to us by right of birth. Instead, it will demand that each of us embrace it, choose it for ourselves, and force our hands to make it happen. It's a bold act of self-determination, urging us to question everything — our assumptions, desires, and the very lives we've built.

To be free, to truly be the selves we are meant to be, is a commitment we must make every day. This is not freedom given by others, but freedom we claim by following our own inner compass.

To live a simple, wild life is to walk toward the unknown — toward what we ourselves long for — rather than what has already been prescribed for us by society. It's an inner journey: breaking free from culture and others' expectations to listen to the whispers of our own hearts and minds.

Living wild means saying no to someone else's envisioning of success or happiness and creating our own.

It's practice — choosing each day to do life in ways that are true to who we are. It means envisioning who we want to be and becoming that person through action, shedding social expectations, and forging our own path.

In this whacky life, we all get to create our own; we all paint on the canvas of our lives.

However, that is not without its own challenges. Life is a constant reminder of the way we are supposed to look, what we are supposed to own, who we are supposed to be. It's easy for all this external pressure to cloud our judgment, to obscure the clear picture of what truly matters to us.

So, the challenge is to stay true to our own desires, to trust ourselves, and to know when it's time to turn down what no longer serves us.

To live authentically, we must often embrace discomfort, uncertainty, and risk. Letting go of others' expectations and trusting our own intuition can be a difficult path. But the reward is immense. We get a powerful sense of peace and satisfaction from leading a life that is true to ourselves — a life in which we don't have to pretend to be someone we're not, don't have to mask our soul with the masks we use to fit in — and just live as ourselves.

Final Challenge: Write a Letter to Your Future Self

Briefly tune in to your future self. Visualize where you see yourself going—not decades from now, but the next chapter of your life. What does that look like? How does it feel? What kind of person have you grown into?

Dear Future Me/Letter to Future You: Write a letter to this future you and describe the life you want for yourself. All the good that's come from it — write it as if it is already happening, as if your dreams, desires, and aspirations have already come to fruition.

In your letter, address the strength, the growth, the courage that you know you possess deep within your soul. Reminisce on the wild, raw life you are creating. What hardships did you face to be where you are now? What decisions have you made that brought you to this point? What have you done to stay true to yourself when it seemed like you couldn't?

When you write, let yourself feel the buzz of excitement and anticipation for what is about to appear. This is the future of you and how you write it.

At the bottom of your letter, pledge to take one step today in that direction. It could be something as simple as establishing a boundary, saying no to something that no longer serves you, or beginning a new project that lights you up.

It's not about "waiting for the right time" — it's about doing it now, in the midst of uncertainty.

When you've completed it, read your letter aloud to yourself.

Hey, listen to those words for a minute. Feel the power and potential in your own voice. You've got it all here on how to build your life.

So, get out there and just take that first step. Not tomorrow, not a week from today — *now*.

Today is the day you start creating the life you have written about, one courageous, true choice at a time. You are the author of your own story, and now it's time to live it.

Dare to be wild. Dare to be authentic. Dare to be free. This is your life to create, and it begins now.